Busy Machines

Tractors

Written by Amy Johnson

Illustrated by Ela Smietanka

Published in 2021 by Windmill Books,
an Imprint of Rosen Publishing
29 East 21st Street, New York, NY 10010

Find us on 

Cataloging-in-Publication Data

Names: Johnson, Amy. | Smietanka, Ela.
Title: Tractors / Amy Johnson, illustrated by Ela Smietanka.
Description: New York : Windmill Books, 2021. | Series: Busy machines
Identifiers: ISBN 9781499485776 (pbk.) | ISBN 9781499485790 (library bound) | ISBN 9781499485783 (6 pack) | ISBN 9781499485806 (ebook)
Subjects: LCSH: Tractors--Juvenile literature.
Classification: LCC TL233.15 J66 2021 | DDC 631.3'72--dc23

Manufactured in the United States of America

CPSIA Compliance Information: Batch BS20WM: For Further Information contact Rosen Publishing, New York, New York at 1-800-237-9932

Tractor power!

On the farm, tractors work busily with other machines to get jobs done.

Hedge trimmer
and VIBRATE...
and CHUG.
Tractor
Trailer

All about tractors

Tractors are very powerful! They are mainly used to pull other farm machines.

The cab is high up so the driver can see all around.
Mudguards stop earth from flying around.
Different machines are joined to the back of the tractor.
Balers make hay, straw, or grass into bales.
Seed drills plant seeds.
Plows turn the soil.
The plow makes rows called furrows as it is pulled through the soil.

Riding high

Tall crops need tall tractors! This **crop sprayer** has extra big wheels so it can travel above plants such as sunflowers.

I drive slowly over the crops.
Steps to reach the cab and engine
There is space underneath so the crops don't get damaged.
Big, chunky tires balance the weight.

Earth work

Before seeds are planted, these machines help to prepare the soil.

Pulverizers pound the soil to loosen it.
Cultivators stir up the soil.
The roller squashes the soil flat.
The disc harrow chops up clumps of earth and uproots weeds.

Sowing Seeds

The fields have been plowed – now they're ready for planting!

Seed drills drop seeds into the ground in rows, then cover them with soil.

The seeds are stored in a large bin. Air from a fan carries them along to each row.
Planters are used to plant bigger seeds.

Busy machines!

Find your favorite
farm machine!

Super machines!

Big Bud is the largest farm tractor in the world. It was built in the U.S. over 40 years ago. It has a powerful engine and huge tires.

Tracked tractors have tough rubber tracks that don't squash the ground as much as wheels.

Harvesters are used in forests to take down trees. They have a long arm that bends and a clawlike grabbing tool.

Time to harvest

Combine harvesters cut crops such as wheat and oats, and then separate the grains from the stalks.

Potatoes bounce along a conveyor belt on the **potato harvester** and into a trailer.

Chute unloads into a trailer

Grass is blown into a chute

Forage harvesters are used to gather grass and corn for animal feed.

Cotton bale

Cotton harvesters pick fluffy white clumps of cotton from their plants.

All about balers

When a field is full of hay bales, it means a **baler** has been hard at work.

Bales are collected by special **bale-handler tractors**. Some can lift six at a time!

3 The back opens and the finished bale rolls out.

Lots of jobs

It takes many kinds of machines to keep a busy farm running.

The boom slides out
to reach high-up things.
Boom lift
Muck spreader
Pickup
truck
Rotary
mower

Tractor tours

Sometimes visitors to the farm can go on tractor rides.

The **milk tanker** is being filled up.

It's feeding time! The **front loader** carries hay for the cows.

Some sheep are being loaded onto the **animal trailer**.
From the **trailer**, visitors have a great view of the farm.
The farmer is using an **all-terrain vehicle** to check on the pigs.

Combine team

When grain is ripe, it takes whole teams of combines to harvest big areas.